# TAKE THE STAGE

Pre to Post Stage Advice, Coaching and

Life Lessons

Tamekia MizLadi Smith

EDU Arts, LLC | www.EduArtsllc.com |
1.800.535.4110

For my grandmother Annie L. Thomas because she taught me

how to stand before anyone!

Edited By: Kathy LaRosa - kathylarosa@yahoo.com

Cover Design & Interior Layout By: RAW Design Studios
www.designzbyraw.com | rawdesignz12@gmail.com

Photo Credit: Cover photos from TED Conference used with permission; taken by Jason Redmond  www.jasonredmond.net




ISBN Number: 978-0-9722368-0-5

## Acknowledgements

To God be the glory for the things he has done. To my family, friends, associates, Dear Poetry, EDU Arts LLC, Nationwide Children's Hospital, TEDx Columbus and TED staff thank you for all your love and support.

# Table of Contents

# BEFORE YOU READ

Throughout this book I refer to the following things quite often and I do not want to assume that everyone knows what they are or what I mean by the term in this context so here are some brief descriptions before you begin to read.

### What is TED?

TED is not a person. It's an acronym that stands for Technology, Entertainment and Design. TED is a nonprofit devoted to spreading ideas, usually in the form of short, powerful talks that are delivered on a red circled shaped carpet in 18 minutes or less.

### What is TEDx?

TEDx was created in the spirit of TED's mission, "ideas worth spreading." It supports independent organizers who want to create a TED-like event in their own community.

### What is meant by "Talk"?

I use the word "Talk" to describe a speech of any length or style. Using this general term allows the reader to apply the advice to whatever type of presentation they are presenting. In instances where I am not referring to the verb the word "Talk" is capitalized.

### What is meant by stage?

The word "stage" represents any space or place a speaker is presenting; from the street corner to the performing arts stage.

# I was born for this!

For the most part this book was written to be a quick reference of advice and a coaching tool for people who either loved or dreaded public speaking. However, true to form, I found myself maneuvering into the world of motivationally speaking directly to those who dare to read. As I wrote, I imagined getting up close and personal with you in an effort to remind you of your brilliance and untapped potential. I even found myself sharing my own experiences on and off the stage. When I decided to title this book "Take The Stage," I meant it from the literal sense of you standing on a physical stage, owning your moment and speaking with confidence, but I also meant it from a figurative sense of you taking your proper position on the stage of life; owning those moments and evolving into whatever it is you are intended to become.

When I was a baby, my grandmother told my father that I was a star; she told him that there was something special about me and that I would achieve great things. As I got older, my father repeated those words in my ear, reinforcing her brave declaration over my life. My deep admiration and love for my grandmother fueled my desire to shine like the star she envisioned. However, my passion and divine purpose in life is the reason why I take the stage. The debate continues as to rather talent is natured or nurtured. A good portion of my life I was raised by my grandmother who by profession was a church musician. I don't recall a time that she didn't have me standing before an audience singing or reciting some kind of speech. My middle school teacher and mentor made sure that I attended a Performing Arts High School and that environment continued to cultivate my talents while keeping me on stages performing in front of people. For those reasons I tend to believe that my natured talent is a product of my nurtured environment.

The pictures on the cover of this book were taken at the 2018 TED Conference in Vancouver, Canada. The paradox of that experience is that nothing about my story qualified me to take that stage – yet everything about my story, my life experiences, *were* my qualifications. I don't believe in coincidences and nothing just happens by chance. While at the conference, I remember sitting in my hotel room and looking at my life in retrospect. I thought of the many times that people said I wasn't talented enough or smart enough or pretty enough. Yet not even their definition of "enough" could stop me from taking my place on that stage and maximizing my moment as an international speaker. The more I looked back, the more I realized that the good, the bad and the ugly experiences of life on and off the stage were all necessary for my growth process.

I know it might sound strange but I imagine that I was belting out a cappella tunes, reciting poetry and delivering Talks while in the womb of my mother. So when I say: "I was born for this" I mean just that! When I take the stage I feel like I come alive.

For me the stage has always been my safe haven. When I'm on the stage, I stand on the shoulders of people that with blood, sweat and tears paved the way so that I might stand there with strength, courage and wisdom.

# Stage 1:

## The Process of Becoming

I will not attempt to define what I mean by "becoming" because I know that it varies from person to person and from moment to moment. The process of "becoming" is like a blank canvas in the hands of an artist; with every swipe and splash of the brush, the manifestation of "WHO" you are becoming begins to take its own form. In the beginning "WHAT" you are becoming is not always identifiable because additional life experiences add and/or take from your formation. Here is the caveat of it all; just when you think that you have completed the process, you will be challenged to become something new because honestly, the process of becoming does not end until you take your last breath.

This writing started off as a TEDx Columbus Talk, written to fit into the 2017 theme of "Trust," but of course the mission attached to that Talk evolved and I desperately wanted to further the conversation that governed the process. I wanted to explore the series of actions or steps that are necessary in order to achieve a particular end. I wanted to make sure that people understood that the "process" can be a lonely road but if you endure it until the end it will all be worth it. The published title of that Talk was "Finding my Voice." I designed the Talk around the metaphor of life being a puzzle with missing pieces; two of those missing pieces were forgiveness and identity. Imagine being able to take the stage with a heart of:

**Forgiveness**

> *"To err is human, to forgive divine."*

> *Alexander Pope*

For years I've heard forgiveness taught on various platforms and I've agreed with its relevance. Nevertheless, when presented with my own opportunities to forgive, I found it to be an unnerving task. My heart was numb and my emotions were admittedly raw with anger. I had recently experienced betrayal and allowed the offense to take root in my heart. When I applied to be a TEDx Columbus 2017 speaker I did not realize how the topic of "trust" would make me examine the authenticity of my forgiveness or lack thereof. As I began to write out my Talk, the missing piece of forgiveness was illuminated. By all means I attempted to avoid the topic but I am not a "creative writer" as much as I am a "conviction writer," therefore I found the topic of forgiveness impossible to avoid.

Often times there seem to be a misunderstanding between the concept of forgiveness and justice. We tend to believe that if we extend forgiveness to the guilty party then we are not receiving our due justice in the situation. However, in order for this to be true, we must also assert that holding unforgiveness in our heart is equivalent to justice which is not true. Getting or not getting justice in a situation has nothing to do with forgiveness. Forgiveness is a standalone entity that has to take place in an individual rather they feel as if justice was served or not. I discovered that forgiveness is more than saying "sorry." Oftentimes people extend or accept an apology without operating in the true realm of forgiveness. There are times that an apology may not be given and you will still be presented with the opportunity to forgive. When I call the act of forgiveness an opportunity, I don't say that vicariously; forgiveness really is an opportunity to free yourself. By definition the act of forgiveness is to pardon; it is the mental and or spiritual process of ceasing to feel resentment, indignation or anger against a person for a perceived offense, difference or mistake. Nevertheless, if we were honest we would admit that forgiveness does not come with amnesia; it does not magically cause you to forget what happened. In some cases forgiveness is instant while in others it is a process that happens over time. Forgiveness sometimes comes with reconciliation and in those cases those that are involved trust that the offense will not happen again. Other times forgiveness comes with separation and in those cases those that are involved trust that the offense is likely to happen again and they choose not to reconnect. One of the issues that I have found with forgiveness is that people will try to use it as a manipulating leash to maintain control over others. They say things like "if you really forgive me then we would reconcile!" That statement could be no further from the truth; sometimes true forgiveness is when you find the strength and the courage to walk away without anger or resentment. Moving on doesn't mean you didn't forgive; it means you simply moved on. Forgiveness is not just a p.i.e.c.e – piece of the puzzle in the process of becoming but it is the p.e.a.c.e – peace within the process. You owe it to yourself to have that peace. So before you take the stage, do something brave and walk onto that stage in the beauty and wholeness of forgiveness.

## Identity and Self – esteem

Although some might view identity and self-esteem as one in the same I like to think of them as fraternal twins because "Identity" deals with "how you perceive yourself" while "self-esteem" deals with "how you value yourself." When I first embraced performing poetry on the stage I went through a huge identity crisis. I began to feel like my hair wasn't poetic enough, my clothes and jewelry was not ethnic enough. I started feeling like I needed to use words like "conscious" so I could sound deep and prolific. I felt like I needed to make new friends in the poetry community in an effort to gain creditability. I needed to become a vegan or a vegetarian and the list went on and on. While there is nothing wrong with any of those things, the truth of the matter is that I didn't need to do any of that in order to embrace who I was becoming.

As it related to self-esteem my understanding of what self-esteem "was not" played a major part in the restoration of my identity. I realized that self-esteem was not about feeling beautiful because there are beautiful people who still lack self-value. Self-esteem is not about feeling superior or elevated social economic status because there are poor people with more self-worth than rich people. My biggest discovery about what self-esteem was not was it's not something that you can depend on others to give you. The word "self-esteem" defines itself in that it is all about having the ability to understand your own, worth and value. Imagine being so comfortable with "who" you are and confident in "what" you can do that you can fearlessly stand center stage in a room filled with amazing people from all walks of life. Imagine being able to communicate so effectively that you leave the audience wanting more. You might ask what self-esteem and identity has to do with taking the stage and I would argue that it has everything to do with it. Most of the time people find it hard to stand before an audience because they lack understanding of who they are and the value in what they have to offer. No matter how good the content of your Talk is, if you are not comfortable with who you are, it will reflect in your presentation and the audience will recognize it.

Tips to restore your identity and improve your self-esteem:

- Write out who you want to become; every day speak those specific things out loud and everyday do something toward the manifestation of your written and spoken confession.

- Be aware of negative self-talk and be intentional about changing your narrative. As soon as you say something negative about yourself write the negative word down and create an acronym of positive words out of that negative word. For example: if you say "I'm sad" write and say something like "I'm **S**atisfied **A**nd **D**etermined!" So now every time I feel sad I say I'm satisfied and determined. (*Oftentimes I use this activity when I'm conducting Confidence Coaching. It really does change the trajectory of my client's self-worth and value.*)

- Stay connected to people that love you; those that speak well of you but will still tell you the truth. Although self-esteem is your personal responsibility, the people around you can affect your "self-perspective". Make sure that you keep company with those who are honest but will celebrate your strength to improve your weakness.

- Place post it notes around your house as reminders to celebrate who you are becoming. For instance, if you want to be an international speaker; write your name and international speaker on a post it note and read it out loud every time you walk past the note.

- Record yourself saying positive affirmations. Your voice is powerful and you need to hear you! Your words are creative and they form the world in which you live in.

## The Fear Factor

*"If they tell me no; it won't be because I didn't give them an opportunity to tell me yes!"*

*Tamekia MizLadi Smith*

This quote has become my motto and every time I go for a new opportunity I look in the mirror and I repeat it to myself. Even your most seasoned speakers feel a since of nervousness before they take to the stage. To be honest, I would worry if I didn't feel those pre-performance jitters that I am accustomed to feeling. While I could give you steps to manage the speaker's' jitters, that is not what this stage is about. In this stage I'm referring to "fear" as that debilitating thief that paralyzes your potential and steals your future. Fear won't even let you apply for a speaking opportunity. Fear will let the incomplete application sit on your desk until the deadline has passed. Fear understands that if you don't face it, it wins by keeping you struck and stunting your growth for lack of movement and progress.

### Fear of Success

It might sound strange but it's true; some people actually fear success – especially those who have only experienced failure.

This type of fear usually expands to every part of your life; so whether consciously or unconsciously, you self – sabotage potential careers and relationship opportunities because failure has become a comfort zone. A person that fears success will apply and submit the application to be selected yet still find a way to destroy future opportunities by their fear that they will lack the ability to continue to succeed.

*Fear of Rejection and Failure*

The fear of rejection says don't even apply; they won't choose you. The fear of failure says if they choose you, you will fail. I have felt and heard both of these statements and they have both been proven wrong in my life by a simple press of the button. I won't give you false hope, there have been things I have applied for and received a rejection letter, but I didn't allow that to stop me from applying for something else.

Are you afraid you might fail? The truth is you might fail at some things; in fact most people that are successful are successful in spite of or because of their failures. For example:

- Oprah Winfrey was fired from her first TV job as an anchor in Baltimore. Imagine if Oprah would have let that one set back stop her from pursuing her dreams.

- Steven Spielberg was rejected twice by the University of Southern California's School of Cinematic Arts; yet his cinematic output has grossed billions of dollars. What if Steven would have allowed those rejection letters to determine his pursuit?

The list goes on and on of successful people that failed or were rejected, but they were also resilient. Most of the books that I've read written by famous people started off with some type of trauma, rejection or epic failure before they were able to achieve success.

When it comes to "taking the stage," the biggest issue is that fear will never allow you to make it to the stage. Fear mutes your voice and never allows you to share your ideas —even if you have them written; fear has made many hide their journals and bury their plans. Unfortunately it is fear that has silenced a generation of brilliant minds. The saddest part is that fear will allow you to watch from the sidelines because fear is a tormentor; it will paralyze you but allow you to see other people living out your dream.

Facing fear means that you are willing to be vulnerable and resilient. When you face fear you press the unmute button; you find your voice and you take the stage. Honestly, I have felt fear and self-doubt every single time that I've applied for anything but I conquered fear by pressing send anyway! So if you are taking to a physical stage or taking your proper position on the stage of life: give it your all because you matter and your visions, your hopes and your dreams matter and they are worth fighting for!

*Finishing*

One day I was teaching a class and as I was giving a demonstration I tripped and fell. My microphone slid across the floor and my hair was out of place and I could literally feel the physical pain from the fall. I remember standing up in front of everyone, dusting myself off, fixing my hair, getting my microphone back and giving people permission to laugh because all I knew is that come what may I was determined to finish. Yes, it was embarrassing, it was unexpected and I felt like it was unfair that it happened to me because falling was not in the plan. But more importantly, quitting wasn't in the plan either; so finishing was my only option. It is popular to say that "failure is not an option" but actually it's the option that millions of people choose every day. Some people have found rest in the seat of discouragement. The truth of the matter is that failure happens to the best of us; but you must understand that failure is what "happened to you" it is not "who you are!" The real issue is never the failure; it's always your response to the failure. A resilient response to failure is accepting accountability, identifying where you went wrong and what you can do better next time. A healthy response to failure is always making sure that you position yourself for another opportunity.

# Stage 2:

## Pre Stage Preparation

Before we go into the stage of submitting applications and or proposals to speak I believe it's essential that we discuss the cleanup process. The delete button on your computer can be a very powerful tool and sometimes in order to grow you have to be willing to let go of the people, places and things that no longer complement or advance your life. The stage of preparation will challenge you to make some difficult decisions because it will present you with the opportunity to change.

### Pre Marketing

Pre Marketing is extremely critical to branding yourself as a speaker because once you hit that "submit" button the reviewers and the powers that be will do their due diligence in researching you. Their search of you will include (but will not be limited to) the internet sites that you provided. It is critical that they find the best representation of who you are within and outside of:

### Social Media

For the most part you cannot control what other people say or post about you but you do have control over what you say or post. Although you are allowed to enjoy your life; a half-naked picture of you extremely intoxicated will most likely not give the best representation of who you are as a professional speaker. When you decide to take the stage, it places you in a public spotlight and that may require that you think twice about what you post. There have been countless examples of people losing their employment or damaging their reputation because of a social media post. A part of your pre marketing efforts should be a good review of the words and or pictures that you have posted and please dismiss the notion of a private post because there is no such thing; if you post it, it's public.

I'll admit that social media has made it easier to advertise to the community of people that follow you. However, marketing is so much more than posting a flyer and receiving online recognition. That's why you should always have an internet presence aside from your social media sites; either your own website or a professionally shared networking site. If applicable, you should also post videos of your previous Talk(s) performed in front of a live audience.

Here are some other pre marketing things to consider:

*An Elevator Pitch

In 30 seconds or in 30 words you should be able to professionally articulate: who you are, what you do and why they need you to do it.

*A Recent Professional Photo

When people ask you to provide a photo it's usually for their marketing material. It is not appropriate to send a selfie, a picture that has been edited to chop out someone else, a picture with distractive background or a low resolution photo. Also as tempting as it might be to send the photo that is 20 pounds lighter and/or 10 years younger, don't do it! If your goal is to take the stage they will eventually see the real you anyway so just send a professionally taken photo that represents the real you.

*A Professionally Typed Biography (bio)

Every speaker should have a general biography available that can easily be edited for different opportunities. Some speakers especially those in academia, research, or medicine have Curriculum vitae (CV) that list in great detail all their research, publications, education and experience. Even if you don't have this information in CV format, having it accessible is critical to streamlining the proposal submission.

*A Speaker's One Sheet

This sheet is usually full color, double sided and easy to read. It gives a brief but detailed overview of who you are, what you do and your contact information. Normally there is a professional picture and listing of your services and or product that is available for purchase. Having this electronically and as a hard copy is a quick way to providing others with information about you.

**Pre Determining**

Pre determining is about analyzing the people, places and things to identify how your Talks will best serve a specific audience.

*Target Markets & Specialty Subjects

Pre determining "who" your target market is and "what" your specialty subjects will be are very essential and knowing this early will save you time and money. If your specialty subject is "Animals" then your target market might be Veterinarians and animal lovers. If your specialty subject is more detailed like "Finding Cures for Animals and Preserving Endangered Species" then your target market may expand to Veterinarians, Research Scientist, Biologist and animal lovers.

You can have more than one subject specialty but don't fool yourself into believing that you can speak on everything. Organizations that seek speakers are usually looking for speakers who are specialists and passionate about the subject not a generalist.

Finding your specialty subject(s) is like finding your voice. It's the thing that you are most passionate about. Once you discover your specialty subjects, focus your time, energy and talents on perfecting that subject(s) and reaching that target market(s).

*Accept or Decline

If you are trying to create a professional speaking career you should require a formal speaker's invitation letter on company letterhead from anyone that asks you to speak. While it is perfectly acceptable to receive this letter via email, it should not come through a social media inbox or verbal agreement. As a speaker you are not obligated to accept every invitation that is extended to you. In most cases you can reserve the right to respectfully decline any invitation at any time without any explanation. I say "in most cases" because some speakers are hired through companies and they are contractually obligated to speak on behalf of that company. In the pre determining stage you have to do your due diligence in researching the organizations that invited you to speak. Knowing the company's reputation, mission, goals and their vision is critical to accepting a speaker's invitation. You should always take the:

*Ethical and Moral Approach

Both ethics and morals relate to "right" and "wrong" conduct and while they are sometimes used interchangeably, they are different: ethics refer to the rules that are provided by an external source (work, school, religion etc.) while morals refer to an individual's own principles regarding what is right and wrong. It is never okay to accept an invitation just because people are willing to pay your fees. Many people have damaged their careers and repetitions for the almighty dollar! If you have to compromise your personal, religious or moral standards in order to fulfill a speaker's obligation you should respectfully decline that invitation. Your ability to maintain your ethical and moral standards should always be the compass for your decision making. That's why in the pre determining stage you should always:

*Seek Before You Speak

The most seasoned speakers must prepare to take the stage. While the process of preparation is different for everyone, it is something that should never be avoided. Every audience is different and they deserve a Talk that is tailored to meet their needs. I can recall the numerous times I have heard speakers deliver a Talk verbatim to different audiences. The sad part is that most of the time it's recorded and the proof is easily accessible through the internet. I'm not saying that you have to deliver a brand new Talk each time you present, but you should make some adjustments to fit the needs of your audience.

Have you ever listened to a speaker and realized that they had no idea what they were talking about? It is the most uncomfortable thing to witness; the rambling of words mixed with the visible nervousness is exhausting to say the least. It quickly becomes apparent that there was a lack of preparation on the speaker's behalf and as an audience member there is nothing you can do to rescue the speaker from this self-destructive moment. Even if the speaker is an articulate presenter, if the content is inaccurate that will always supersede their delivery techniques. Before you even begin the writing process you should:

*Seek Wisdom

Wisdom is the quality of having experience, knowledge, and good judgment. When a Talk is not written and or delivered in wisdom it can ruin a person's reputation and character. Wisdom will instruct you on what, when and how to say or not say something. You will never possess all the wisdom in the world but sometimes as you seek wisdom what you find is people who are wiser, at which point you should:

*Seek Counsel

Counsel is advice and instruction; seeking counsel from people who are more experienced then you is a product of wisdom. Seeking council allows you to get clarity and ask clarifying questions. Counsel allows you to hear a different perspective and offers you guidance on which way you should go in your writing and or presenting. You should also:

*Seek Understanding

Understanding is about doing your research, reading and studying beyond that which you will present. You don't have to present all you know but you should know more than you present. Oftentimes after you deliver a Talk it is common for people to desire to further the conversation. If this happens and people realize that your understanding of the subject matter goes no further than what you presented, it could discredit you and harm your reputation. The criticism of others can hurt but you should always:

*Seek Constructive Criticism

Constructive criticism helps to improve your skills; it promotes further advancement. Therefore being open to constructive criticism is essential to the growth of a speaker because it allow them to remain teachable.

## Motivational Moment

*I remember when I was preparing to speak at the TED Conference; it was my first video rehearsal and the head of TED, Chris Anderson, along with other curators and coaches were going to be a part of the rehearsal. Chris Anderson started off praising me; he told me how great I was in New York and how pleased he was to have me as a speaker for the conference. In the same moment he and others begun to rip my Talk apart; they told me I was all over the place, suggested that I remove parts and shift others. At first it was daunting because I really thought my Talk in its current state was great! However, as I implemented the changes and reviewed my final Talk, I realized how instrumental their constructive criticism was to the development of my Talk. People that care about your growth will always tell you the truth and give you the tools you need to develop and excel.*

**The Writer**

Let's examine what type of writer you are because that usually determines the way in which you will deliver your Talk:

- The Free Style Writer

  This type of writer can sit down and write with no structure at all. They know the subject that they want to talk about and they simply allow the words to land on the paper. During the editing phase the free style writer will set up some type of order to their Talk. This type of writer can usually deliver their Talk with little or no notes and they are normally inspirational or motivational type speakers.

- The Notes Writer

  This type of writer takes copious notes and they usually deliver their Talks by read their notes verbatim. Their style of delivery is usually mostly appreciated in academia or in lecture type settings.

- The Bullet Point Writer

  This type of writer generally only needs a few bullet points to steer the delivery of their Talk. They are usually seasoned speakers and experts in their field of study.

- The Brainstorm Writer

  This type of writer plays by all the rules; they use graphs and charts to organize their Talks; they pre write, write, revise, edit and repeat that process several times if necessary. Their method of delivery is usually very strategic and well thought out.

## Pre Writing

*"I dance the tangle in a web of words and my mission is to extract the right ones; words that fall from my lips and land on your heart as a seed and produce a great harvest."*

*Tamekia MizLadi Smith*

In this section we will discuss the words, the Talk and the audience:

## The Words

We live in a world that is filled with a diversity of words, languages and dialects. These words have the power to paint vivid pictures by describing things like the element of touch, the beauty of sight and the uniqueness of sound. As human beings we use written and or spoken words as a form of communication. From a grammatical perspective there is a "right" and a "wrong" way to construct words into a proper sentence. Nevertheless, the writing in this section is not about sentence structure; it's about finding the right words, to convey the right Talk, to the right audience.

*Ethics in your Content:

It is important that you avoid distorting content; be honest and thoroughly research facts and figures. Remember we live in the age of technology; while you are yet speaking, your audience may simultaneously be fact checking you with their phones in an effort to discredit your talk before you even leave the stage.

Make sure you note when you are quoting someone and in some cases make sure you get permission and/or cite when you are using others' materials. Avoid all fallacies; this is an argument that is based on false inferences. Also be ethical in your use of an emotional appeal to avoid exploiting the vulnerable population or inducing fear.

*Word Selection:

When I was younger, I remember singing the jingle that said "stick and stones may break my bones but words will never hurt!" As an adult I now know that on many levels those words are not true! Words can and will hurt you! Not only will they hurt you but they can also hurt others that hear them. When selecting the right words consider the following:

- Slang – Using slang in some environments will make you look and or sound less intelligent.

- Cursing – Even if it's not a religious or a children's event, using curse words may not be appreciated and/or appropriate.

- Deep Metaphors – While this may be received with praise at a poetry or writer's events, people outside of those creative circles might just find you weird and confusing.

*Avoid Stereotypes, Scapegoating and Generalizations

Stay clear of these things unless your goal is to offend and or be controversial. When words like "everybody, all the time and never" are used, they are normally not true. For example: *"Everybody in the whole world loves pizza; they eat it all the time; therefore you can never go wrong with pizza."* That whole statement is false because of the word selection. Another way to say it is: *"Some people love pizza and they eat it a lot; you can almost never go wrong with ordering pizza for people that love it."*


## *Certain Jokes

There is nothing better than a Talk that lands the perfect joke at the perfect time and there is nothing worse than the most offensive or vulgar joke said at the worst time. Jokes that reference things like race, gender or religion in a negative way may be taken offensively; even if you "meant" it as a joke.


## *Personal Agendas

I think the name alone says it all: "personal," which means that you should probably keep it personal and not share it with the audience. It's never okay to push your "personal" agenda on an unsuspecting audience. *For example: If you are being asked or paid to talk about the environment; it is not acceptable to use that moment or platform to talk about something other than the environment.* Personally, I have seen it happen before and not only offended the organizers of the event, but the participants felt cheated.

## *Bias

A bias is a prejudice in favor of or against one thing, person, or group compared with another usually in a way that's considered to be unfair.
There are two types of biases

- Conscious bias (also known as explicit bias) and

- Unconscious bias (also known as implicit bias)

Whether we admit it or not, in one way or another, most people have a bias toward something. However, the goal is to face those biases before you speak in an effort not to present them within your Talk.

*Consider Evidence

Your words should consist of evidence based research and/or relevant personal experience. Different types of Talks require different levels of research, statistics and/or data to persuade or engage the audience. However, a Talk without any research and or relevant personal experience is simply a Talk filled with your opinions. Sometimes citing evidence can increase the creditability of your Talk. It shows that you studied the subject and that you are prepared. Using any known facts or current events can help you connect with your audience.

**The Talk**

Personally, I believe the goal of every writer should be to present in a way that the visual, auditory, reading/writing, and kinesthetic learners will be able to relate to their Talk. The basic 4 types of Talks are:

- Informative Talk

    o Purpose – to give your audience thought provoking information

- Persuasive Talk

    o Purpose - to convince your audience to agree, buy, do or believe something

- Demonstrative Talk

    o Purpose – to explain or to show how something is done or works

- Entertaining Talk

    o Purpose – to express a message creatively usually through a joke or short story

The different types of Talks can be used individually or collectively to accomplish your ultimate goal. You do not have to stick to one type of Talk; the most serious messages can still be entertaining in an effort to convey the importance of that message. However, be aware that too much of anything can become convoluted and you can easily lose your desired effect. For example, too many jokes can make it appear as if you don't take the subject seriously unless you are a comedian and laughter is the general purpose of your Talk.

## The Audience

You should always consider your audience because after all, without them there would be no opportunity or reason for you to take the stage. One of the most essential things that a speaker should know is the purpose, goals and/or the central idea of the event in which they are speaking. You can be the best speaker in the world but if your content does not reflect the desired outcome of the event your speaking is in vain. It is also important to have some demographic information on your audience like age, culture and/or education level. This type of information will prevent you from speaking over or under the audience comprehension. You'll never be able to impact people that can't understand you or those that feel as if you are insulting their intelligence.

## Preparing the Talk

A speaker should construct a Talk according to the guidelines given by the organizer, including a timeframe. For instance, if you were given a certain amount of time, construct your Talk with that time limit in mind. The content of a 10 minute Talk will be different from that of a 90 minute keynote Talk. However, the construction of it may be similar.

Talk Construction:

10 minute Talk time structure:

- Introduction – 1 minute

- Main Idea Statement – 1 minute

- 3 points or more to support the Main Idea – 2 minutes for each point totaling 6 minutes

- Recap Conclusion – 2 minutes

- 90 minute Talk time structure:

- Introduction – 10 minutes

- Main Idea Statement – 10 minutes

- 3 points or more to support the Main Idea – 20 minutes for each point totaling 60 minutes

- Recap Conclusion – 10 minutes

## TALK SURVEY 1

Let's look at how I constructed the talk I presented at the DISCOVERYx event located at Nationwide Children's Hospital.

**Title: Overcoming Social Determinates through Mentoring**

Year: 2016

Time: 10 Minutes

You Tube: https://www.youtube.com/watch?v=OY4Y6tlVeeQ

### The Introduction

The introduction was an original poem entitled "What if?" I wrote the poem as if "children" and "butterflies" were one in the same. Within the poem I ask the question "what if they never become butterflies?" The question was presented so the audience could think about the disparity of children never getting an opportunity to fully bloom because of the Social Determinates that they face. Here is why this construction was creative and important:

- The Talk was done at a children's hospital and their logo was butterflies – whenever you are doing a Talk for a company try to incorporate, create or say something that is tailored specifically for that opportunity.

- The poem connected the problem of Social Determinates to the Health Equity or the lack thereof as it relates children.

**What is Social Determinates?** Within the introduction after the poem I defined the subject of Social Determinates; never assume everyone knows what you are talking about always do a quick definition review.

**Main Idea State:** In this Talk, my main idea statement was a picture of a person in poverty versus a person that grew up in wealth. I thought this picture was unique because it showed how poverty and wealth can be passed down from one generation to the next.

**Sharing my story and how it relates to Social Determinates** – Sharing my story was the heart of the matter; speakers talk about things all the time because their research or education affords them the opportunity but very rarely do they have the hands on experience. Sharing your personal experience with your audience allows you to connect.

**Introduction to Mentoring:** Just like I defined Social Determinates I took some time to define Mentoring. Any subject that you mention in your title should be defined and explored in your Talk.

**My Mentor:** I was very vulnerable in my Talk in that I spoke on the domestic violence that I witnessed in my home growing up and the death of my mentor via domestic violence.

**My Mentees:** I shared how my mentor's influence changed the trajectory of my life and how because of this, I now mentor young ladies to make a difference.

**Conclusion:** I went back to a recite a part of the poem that summed up my whole Talk:

*"Each one - should teach one - should love one -*

*should mentor at least one!"*

My purpose of the Talk was to encourage people to mentor at least one child so they can fully develop into beautiful butterflies that overcame Social Determinates. Now let's survey a longer keynote address Talk done at United Way:

**TALK SURVEY 2**

**Title: The 5 star Approach to Mentoring Healthy Neighborhoods**

Year: 2016

Time: 90 Minutes

Introduction Poem – I did not customize a poem for this Talk but I did use a previously written poem that fit into the theme. After the poem I explore the principle of mentoring by answering the question of "What is Mentoring?" because I had more time I was able to give example and further explore what becoming a mentor for your community looks like. After the introduction I selected the following 4 health issues:

- HIV/ AIDS Epidemic

- Mental Health Crisis

- Obesity

- Infant Mortality

I talked about each issue in detail by citing statistic and related research. I then introduced the 5 Star Approach:

- Attitude

- Advocacy

- Academia

- Anti-Violence

- Arts and Culture

I spoke at length on how each point could create healthier neighborhoods. In conclusion, I spoke about implementing the plan and momentum techniques.

# Stage 3:

## The Submission

As a speaker some opportunities will come to you and others will require that you submit an application or a speaker's proposal. The submission process can be a daunting task because the world of public speaking is just as competitive as the job market. Most organizations that hire speakers have whole committees that will review the speaker's submission; within this vetting process amongst other things the committee is looking for the best speakers to meet or exceed their desired outcomes for their audience.

Answer the Call

Different organizations that host events are always looking for speakers so they'll release what is called a "Call for Speakers." Do not try to answer every call; only submit a proposal for opportunities that are within your specialty topic and target market. The hosting organization will normally give you their guidelines for the proposal. However, the following items are normally requested so having them handy will save you time:

- Your proposal title - Consider your audience and create a title that they will look at and want to attend.

- A simple statement that describes your idea– the reviewer cares about how brilliant you are but they want to articulate that in as little words as possible. In some cases there are hundreds of proposals submitted, so keep it short and powerful.

- Type of session (is it a keynote, breakout session or a workshop)

- Presenters Information (name, email, website, phone number)

- Brief speaker's biography or detailed CV information

- Brief description of your proposed session, abstract or a session outline

- Deliverables - What will the participant benefit from attending your session

- 3-5 learning objectives that are written to the participants

- Credibility - A list and or a link of previous Talks and references


Auditions

Submitting an application is a little different but having the above list handy is still relevant.

- Although most applications use online forms, some still require that you type and submit via email. In those cases use a normal font like "Times New Roman or Arial", 1.5 spacing and bold the subtopics.

- Avoid slang, check your spelling and grammar and if possible, let someone else proofread and edit your submission. The reviewer will assume that you talk the way you write.

- Follow the given guidelines - for example, if you are asked to submit 100 words or less; submit 100 words or less.

When asked to audition in person:

- Although they are not as popular anymore, in person auditions still happen. Make sure you are on time, dressed appropriately and know your material. Unlike a video you cannot stop and do it over without looking like you are not prepared.

- Be conscious of your behavior the whole time you are at the audition site because your audition starts with your first interaction and it ends with your last one. Think it not strange that being rude to the receptionist can cause you to miss out on an opportunity. Treat everybody with respect as if they all determine if you are selected.

When asked to submit a video:

- Remember to dress the part; it's a visual tool and the reviewers will judge you by your appearance.

- Practice before you record to avoid wasting time or sounding like you are reading; relax and be natural.

- Be conscious of the scenery that you record in; avoid noisy, messy and cluttered areas. Make sure your scene reflects the message you are trying to convey. For example: Do not shoot your video in a graveyard unless you are talking about death and trying to make a point.

- If they ask for a 30 second or a 2 minute video do not go over that time; in most cases that will automatically disqualify you.

- If possible, let someone else record you so you can focus on your audition. However, if no one else is available do a selfie video.

## Motivational Moment

*My video submission for the TED New York auditions was a selfie video and with that I was selected as one of the 13 finalists so please do not allow the lack of help to stop you. Also remember they are asking for a video in part because they want to see you and how you speak. If you really believe in what you are saying, create a perfect sales pitch and make the reviewers believe it, too. Make sure your voice, your message and your confidence is congruent in your video. Normally you'll have less than 90 seconds to make the reviewers love you and want more.*

*Go for it!*

# Stage 4:

## The Performing Arts

Performing Arts is an art form in which an artist uses their voice, instrument or body to convey artistic expression. Incorporating this type of expression in a Talk is not common but when implemented properly can be very impactful. Canadian communication theorist Marshall McLuhan said, "Anyone who tries to make a distinction between education and entertainment doesn't know the first thing about either". I have always been an advocate of educating through the arts and I try to demonstrate that every time I take to the stage. However, performing arts is not every one's gift and I would strongly suggest that if it is not your gift then avoid trying to incorporate it unless you are willing to share the stage with someone that can demonstrate the arts while you execute the Talk. I've literally sat in audiences where people announced that they could not sing yet they still decided to sing before their Talk and honestly, it was an epic fail. Not only did it distract from the message, but it damaged the speaker's reputation.

Don't Over Do It!

My original Talk at the TED Conference consisted of:

- a poem

- 1 fiction story

- 1 true story and the Talk

That was way too much to cram into 9 minutes; my coaches suggested that I eliminated the poem and make some other changes. In retrospect, I'm glad that I implemented their suggestions because in doing so it allowed the audience to focus on the heart of the matter which was displayed through the story and supported through the Talk. As a Creative, I know how tempting it can be to showcase every gift you possess but resist the urge and focus on the primary goal of the Talk. With that being said, it is also important that you don't underestimate the power of incorporating:

## The Art of Storytelling

The benefit of creating fictional stories in a Talk is that you can be creative and make the character fit into the content of your Talk. The unbeneficial part is that if it is not delivered right it can be confusing and less effective. Implementing the power of education and performing arts to convey a message is the core of my work because I understand that people learn in various ways. And while the art of storytelling is not a new thing, it is often under-utilized or poorly executed. I believe whole heartedly that whether you are telling a true story or a story of fiction, if executed properly you can reach your audience. When creating your story here are some fundamental things you need to do:

- **Create an opportunity for the audience to care.**

  The only way you can do this is by making sure that your audience can make the connection between your story and your Talk. If there is a disconnection as to why you told the story the audience will not understand why they need to care. Before you tell the story on stage tell a few friends and or family members the story. Ask them what they got from your story and how they feel after hearing it. If it does not deliver your intended results, go back and rewrite the story.

- **Create an unforgettable character.**

  Give your character a name so people can talk about it long after you leave the stage. Even if you are telling a true story, describe yourself in an unforgettable way. If you connected your Talk and your character properly not only will the audience remember your character but they'll remember your message. In stories of fiction, create a voice for the character that is different than your voice. Making a distinction between you and the character will help the audience to understand when you are shifting from storytelling to your Talk.

- **Let your words paint your scene.**

  The audience cannot be left to assume anything because that leaves too much room for error. A great storyteller will use their words to take the audience to the setting of the story seamlessly.

- **Tell the story in chronical order.**

  Make sure your story is not all over the place. If the audience gets confused they will stop listening and it will be hard if not impossible to get them to reconnect.

- **Make sure you have a strong finish.**

  Have you ever watched a movie and hated the ending? You tend to believe that the whole movie was a failure. People are waiting for your big finish and if it is weak the audience might sum the whole Talk up as weak.


## TALK SURVEY 1

**TED Conference**

Date: April 2018 Conference in Vancouver, Canada

go.ted.com/tamekiamizladismith

Within my Talk at the TED conference I created a fictional character name "Miz Margaret" to better engage my audience. I thought incorporating a fictional story would not only entertain but also educate the audience. Including this story was a success because it followed the guidelines mentioned above:

- It created an opportunity for the audience to care. The story was tailored for the Talk. Miz Margaret was seasoned in her position and was somewhat resistant to change. The story allowed the audience to be mindful of people like Miz Margaret within their organization and to find ways to engage and/or change their perspective.

- Miz Margaret was an unforgettable character because she had an attitude that the audience could relate to personally or knew someone like her in real life.

- I painted the scene with my words by saying "Miz Margaret had been a front desk specialist for over 20 years in a hospital setting."

- I told the story in chronological order making it easy to follow; after describing the setting, stating the problem and conflict. I allow the Talk to offer the solution as a way of connecting the Talk with the story.

- I made sure there was a strong finish. The ending was perfect in that it went back to the punchline of "bring food to meetings." This was another thing people could relate to and many people that lead meetings as a part of their job joked with me after my Talk that they will now make sure that they bring food to their meetings.

## Telling a True Story

When telling a true story sometimes reality can be stranger than fiction. There are many things to consider when you decide to take the stage and tell your story. The very first thing to consider is your audience and in today's world with all the technology it is important that you understand that your audience could be at any minute anyone with access to a computer or a phone. People will "Go Live" without your permission and share a video of you without your consent.

With that being said, I will now refer to your audience as your "intended" audience, which are the people that you either agreed and/or were paid to speak before. There is a difference between telling your story versus telling your business. I remember attending an event and the speaker was a well-known charismatic speaker; she started to tell a rather lengthy story about her new husband. The story included tidbits and jokes about how she was sexually satisfied. Because of her popularity most of the people in the room thought it was funny or cute but I was extremely confused and thought it was unnecessary and unwise. I felt like she used valuable time to tell her business and although it entertained some, it helped no one. If telling your true story does not benefit or help your intended audience – do not tell it. If it has nothing to do with the topic you have been asked to speak about – do not share it. As a speaker it is important that you do not build a speaking career by telling your story only. In doing this you limit yourself, your audience and your gift. When you have determined that it is appropriate to tell your story you should answer the following questions:

### Are you really ready to share your story?

Telling a true story can be a pool of mixed emotions for the storyteller and it is completely normal to get a little chocked up while telling your story. However, becoming extremely emotional and falling apart in the middle of your Talk leaves your audience to believe that you are fragile. Sharing your story when you are not emotionally free from the trauma will not help anyone. Not being ready to tell your story does not make you weak but allows you to acknowledge the fact that there is still some areas that you may still need healing.

### Why are you sharing your story?

This is probably the most important question to answer because when you know "why" everything else falls into place.

Answering "why" presents you with an opportunity to check your motives. If you are sharing your story to:

- Be famous

- Get sympathy or attention

- Expose or embarrass someone else

Then your motives are off and you will probably do more harm than good;because that harm will most likely be to yourself.

Nevertheless, you can answer the question of "why" by answer the following questions:

- What is the real purpose in sharing your story?

- What would you like the audience to experience from sharing your story?

**Who does your story involve?**

Sometimes your story involves other people either directly or indirectly. For example, your story may affect your children even if they were not born when the events took place. You should have a conversation with people that are directly or indirectly affected by you telling your story before you tell it. I remember engaging my parents in the "why" I was telling my story because I knew that in some ways it did not paint a perfect picture of them as parents. I explained to them "why" I needed to share my story and "who" I felt it would help. When I engaged them in that conversation it opened up an opportunity for them to share with me where they were in life at that time. This information did not change my experiences but it allowed me tell my story with a sense of compassion and consideration. I know that this is not always possible. I know that in some cases people will not be able to have a civilized conversation no matter what technique they attempt to use. So while it is important to consider those people and their feelings, it should not stop you from telling your story. Understand that your story is your perspective; it is your truth as you know it and this will probably be challenged by others. Everybody will not celebrate your courage to tell your story. Some people will be mean, critical, and even accuse you of lying or attention seeking. Being ready to tell your story is also about being ready for the potential backlash.

## What and how much do you want to share?

Once you have settled in your heart that you want to share your story, next determine "how" you will tell your story and "how much" of your story you will tell. You do not have to be reckless in the telling of your story.

Answer this question: Can you tell the story without calling out names and destroying relationships?

Sometimes you can, other times you can't. However, there is a wisdom in being discrete that has preserved many families as well as allowed the victim to heal and in some cases extend forgiveness.

When you take to the stage with your story make sure there is balance. I have heard Talks where people had 10 minutes to speak and for the first 8 minutes they talked about the trauma sparing no grizzly details and in the last 2 minutes they talked about how they were liberated and free never realizing that they just traumatized their audience.

Effective storytelling is about balance and making sure the "why" you are telling your story is accomplished. If you want your story to strength the audience and be viewed as victorious and not a victim, you should spend more time talking about how you overcame what you went through. It's not okay to make your audience a second victim to your trauma, be a responsible speaker; if you have a short timeframe make sure you allot enough time to convey the whole message and purpose of telling your story.

## TALK SURVEY 2

Within my TEDx Columbus Talk I told a true story. Let's survey the construction of this Talk:

**Title: Finding My Voice**

Date: 2017

You                                                      Tube:
https://www.youtube.com/watch?v=6sNE6GWaNyk

Introduction – I started off with an original poem that was written for this Talk that explored how everything has a process before it comes to its fullness. I told the true story of how my very first poem was a suicide letter I was leaving to my family and friends until I realized that it rhymed and I could write poetry.

I begin to build the body of the Talk by exploring: What prevented me from being just another number in the suicide statistics? I asserted that it was:

The Arts – became my voice

My Mentors – were my influence

The World of Academia – became my resources

I likened the process of human life to that of a puzzle with missing pieces. I asserted that that my 3 missing pieces which became my 3 main points were; forgiveness, identity and love:

The Process of **Forgiveness**

Forgiving with no apology

Reconcile Forgiveness or Separation Forgiveness

The Process of **Identity**

How I lost myself

How mentors help me find myself

The Process of **Love**

Healing from past

I concluded the Talk with the process of "trusting the process" and finding the strength to "become" against all odds.

# Stage 5:

## The Rehearsal

I have a love/hate relationship for structured rehearsals. I love the fact that the rehearsal is a great place to mess up because you know you have another opportunity to get it right. Nevertheless, I had one rehearsal that went extremely well and ironically enough the actually performance didn't go so well. So in my mind a "good" rehearsal will mess up my performance. Although I know that's not necessarily true I can't seem to make a disconnection between the two. However, my personal rehearsal time is different. I usually record the structure of my Talks and listen to it periodically. I'm known for having post it notes all over my mirrors and it's not unusual for me to be up at 3am practicing any and everything. When I was in Canada I realized that this behavior didn't sit well with my hotel neighbor; I'd been up rehearsing and apparently I was too loud and rehearing with such aggression that there was a knock at my door and a woman asking me to "please be quiet!" By the time I looked out the peephole all I could see was a woman marching away from my door in her night grown. I felt so bad but I laughed so hard because I really didn't realize I was that loud.

### Tour the Venue

If you have the opportunity to tour the venue by all means take advantage of it. This gives you a moment to become familiar with your surroundings. This will also give you something to connect with your audience about when you deliver your Talk. You can note your travel time, check out the parking structure, determine where to get food and rest rooms are located.

## The Stage

The rehearsal is the perfect time to get a feel for the stage, a sound check, a microphone fitting, experience the lights, and check your ability to see the screen and or the teleprompter if applicable. It was during the rehearsal at TED New York that I realized that the teleprompter was smaller than I expected, I had too many words on my slides and my PowerPoint presentation colors did not work well with the cameras. This made me nervous but I was grateful that I discovered it during the rehearsal and not during the performance.

## The Wardrobe, Hair and Makeup

Shakespeare said it best when he said "to thine own self be true." The stage will brand you and whether you like it or not, image is everything; so consequently, your hair and the clothes you wear tell a story before you even open your mouth to speak. If you don't wear an expensive weave or clothes on a regular basis don't do it for the camera. Don't allow people to fall in love with an image you can't maintain.

## Wardrobe

Always have a backup plan because wardrobe malfunctions are real. This could mean that the beautiful outfit you decided to wear might conflict with the lights and cameras; so you'll need to have something else ready to wear. Take a picture in the clothes that you want to wear. Oftentimes you don't know how great or horrible you look in something until you see a picture of yourself in it.

## Hair and Makeup

Depending on the event budget there may be hair stylist and or makeup artist on site to assist you. However, this doesn't always work out. As it relates to makeup, taking a basic class wouldn't be a bad idea just in case you have to do your own. A lot of times when I travel I know that my stylist cannot travel with me so I prepare to do my own hair. However, when that service is provided by the organizers I like to take advantage of it. I remember asking the three stylists on site if they had experience with doing "short relaxed black hair" and I wasn't being factious. I know that I was a minority at this event and I wasn't sure if they had the proper products for my hair. However, when one of the stylists replied that she had a "black boyfriend" I knew I would have to prepare to do my own hair. I laughed at the comparison because I knew she meant well despite the fact that one thing had nothing to do with the other. The only problem was that this was not the rehearsal but the actual day of the Talk. I began to panic as I searched for a space to do my hair because I did not have enough time to go back to my hotel. This was definitely something I could have and should have found out at the rehearsal. The good news is that I was able to set up my own mini hair salon back stage and my hair was done in time for my Talk. However, I know that everyone don't have the ability to do that so having a backup plan is essential. The day of your Talk is not the time to try something new because if you hate your hair and makeup it will affect how comfortable you feel when you take the stage. Also remember there are cameras and people are taking pictures and that media could show up anywhere at any time so you want to look your best.

# Stage 6:

## Lights Camera Action!

Finally, the moment that you have been waiting for has arrived and your nerves are racing, palms are sweaty and you'll be glad when it's over so you can do it all over again; at least that's how I feel each time I take the stage. Keep in mind that for some people in your audience you'll be making a first impression, some may be adoring fans while others are unfortunate foes. The notion that your "brand" is only your image or marketing materials is a myth. As a speaker your brand is your attitude, your response, your personality and your behavior both on and off the stage.

### Time Will Tell

You might be surprised by the things that time will tell you. When taking the stage it is important that you understand it is only symbolically yours to take during the time that is allotted to you. It is so essential that in your rehearsals you make sure you are keeping proper time. When people disregard their allotted time, they reveal their true self; they show others that they are dismissive and disrespectful. I'll never forget the time I witnessed this and unfortunately I'll always remember the person that committed this very unprofessional act. For the purpose of confidentiality, we'll just call the speaker Mary. There were 5 speakers scheduled to speak for an event and Mary was scheduled to be the first speaker but she was running late and did not get to the event on time. The event coordinator decided to start the event without Mary. Once Mary got to the event she walked straight up to the front where the coordinator was seated to see if she could still deliver her Talk. From the body language alone you could tell that an argument was about to ensue. I learned later that in an effort to prevent a scene the coordinator went ahead and let Mary do her Talk. Mary was a great speaker but most of the participants could not receive from her because they had witnessed her behavior. Not only did it seem like she forced her way back into the program but she also took more time once she received that opportunity to speak. Everyone was shocked and word got around quickly to never invite Mary to speak at your event. This example goes to show how talent is never enough when your character is in disarray and you are not respectful of others. Which now leads us into the conversation on:

## Self – Presentation

The topic of self – presentation refers to how people attempt to present themselves to control or shape how others (called the audience) view them. It involves expressing oneself and behaving in ways that create a desired impression. Self-presentation is part of a broader set of behaviors called impression management. (http://psychology.iresearchnet.com/social-psychology/self/self-presentation/)

The topic of self – presentation could have been discussed in the pre-stage section because actually self – presentation happens before you take the stage. In fact, once you are on the stage people already perceive that they know you by your behaviors, social media, previous Talks and/or products that you have already produced. This preconceived notion of who you are places you in a very interesting position. For example, I remember when I was on my way to speak at the TED Conference in Canada and with excitement the lady that was seated next to me on the plane (who was also a speaker) said: "I know you! I saw your TEDx Columbus Talk; you were amazing!" I laughed and thanked her for her compliments at the same time I felt a mini anxiety attack forming. Here she was, a complete stranger who felt as if she "knew" me. In that moment I felt the fear of success trying to rise up because instantly I begin to question if my new Talk would be as good as she had perceived my previous Talk to be. I wondered if others attending the conference had viewed my previous Talks and had that same expectation of me. It wasn't until I took full control of my thoughts that I regained control of the moment and felt a sense of peace. I had to remind myself of my original school of thought which was that every time I'm graced with an opportunity to take the stage I completely die to the notion of competition. I don't even compete with myself; I don't focus on doing better than anyone; I simply focus on doing my best. I owe it to my current audience to be mindful in the moments that I have with them and I can't do that being engulfed by yesterday's successes or failures.

## Stage Presence

People will critique you; they'll make hasty generalizations that are based solely on their perception of you. And as you begin to deliver your Talk, everything you do or say can and will be held against you in the court of public opinion. Sometimes those opinions are flattering and encouraging while other times they are heartbreaking and discouraging. The one thing you'll never be able to do is to take away another person's right to form and voice their opinion of you. As long as you can accept that you can manage the moments on stage and in life.

A lot of the advice in this section depends on the type of Talk you are giving, your audience and your desired affects. With that being said, there are no real general rules that cover the proper way to deliver the various types of Talks. So when it comes to stage presence ask yourself the following question:

How do I want my message to be perceived by my audience?

Believe it or not the answer to this question will determine other decisions like your attire, makeup, hair and the way in which you sit or stand when you take the stage.

*For Example*

*If you are a college professor delivering a Talk to colleagues you may want to be perceived as polished and professional. So you would dress and speak accordingly. However, if you are in a community theater and you are delivering a monologue of a lady with a mental health issue; you want your audience to feel the effects of a mental health illness and you would certainly give this presentation more drama and expression.*

Imagine for a moment that the audiences got mixed up and the mental health monologue was delivered to unsuspecting college professors. I believe the police and medical professionals would be called to the scene immediately. Nevertheless, when people don't master stage presence and understand the power of connecting with their audience, it leaves a strange sense of discomfort. Managing the moment is about recognizing what is needed and delivering in that moment. It is also about choosing the proper method of delivery that's why it important to have:

## Diversity in Delivery

We've already discussed the importance of knowing some demographic information of your audience; now let's examine the importance of diversifying your delivery techniques. I've been told that when I'm on the stage I become a totally different person. I take that as a compliment because my on-stage presence should be tailored for that moment. It would be quite confusing if I presented to a room of investors as if I was performing poetry on a stage. Knowing your audience means having the ability to change your delivery technique. Before you present ask yourself:

How does the group I'm presenting to learn?

For example, my delivery technique changes when I'm talking to a group of teenagers versus executives. I don't change because I respect one group more than the other; I change because I know one group learns differently than the other.

## Manage the Moment

*"You can make a small message big or a big message small; it's all
about how you manage the moments that you are given."*

*Tamekia MizLadi Smith*


Instant                    Content                    Change
I have been on the stage and said something that wasn't in my
notes and it went extremely well. However, I've also said
something not in my notes and wished I hadn't because it took
me in a direction that I didn't intend to go. And transitioning
back to my original point became an obstacle. Managing the
moment of instant content change can be challenging. Early in
my speaking career I took a lot of opportunity for the exposure
and in doing so I lacked professionalism and proper
preparation. There was a time that I agreed to speak for an
event but I didn't do my due diligence regarding researching
the audience and or the organization. I went prepared to speak
on one topic and realized once I was there that my topic had
nothing to do with the event; in fact my topic would probably
offend the audience. At that time having access to the web
wasn't as phone accessible as it is now. I remember asking
someone for paper and a pen to write with; I was so upset with
myself for not preparing properly. I was able to pull something
together in time to present but I remember never wanting to
feel that feeling again or take the responsibility of my audience
for granted.

Now as a speaker there are moments I'm presented with the
opportunity to "go off script" – meaning I can take the liberty of
going in a different direction. If I'm speaking and I sense the
audience is confused or bored, I view that as an opportunity to
clarify a point in that moment. I am very conscious of the fact
that not every speaker has the ability to maneuver in this
manner. What I called an opportunity might be another
speaker's worst nightmare. At the slightest change or
distraction some speakers totally fall apart, they go blank and
can't remember their Talk. In those unfortunate moments it can
seem as if finding your next thought takes forever. Admitting a
brain freeze or loss of thought is not a crime; most audiences
will be kind and let you collect your thoughts. In those

moments if you let your mind go to a place of defeat you can destroy a Talk that could have been recovered. In managing the moment, you should also consider:

## Posture, Pace & Visual Aids

*Posture*

The particular way in which you sit or stand.

- A power pose is a hypothesis in psychology that says that by assuming a» powerful «posture, subjects can induce positive hormonal and behavioral changes. So rather you choose to sit or stand during your presentation do it with confidence and strike a power pose or two.

- Own your position on that stage! In that moment, it belongs to you and you alone. Create a welcoming atmosphere and engage your audience to share in your experience.

- People can sense when you lack confidence and they can smell the scent of your fear. Practice some power poses in the mirror and remind yourself that you are beautiful or handsome, brilliant and intelligent.

*Pace*

Talk at a consistent speed, not too fast – not too slow.

- Invite your audience to experience your words by making every word count. Let them follow your story, get the punch line of your joke and or connect with their emotions. You can have the right words but the pace in which you deliver them can determine if you connect with the audience.

*Visual Aids*

What you give the audience and what they see on the screen can either help or hinder your presentation. Visuals matter. Using unreadable charts and outdated data can take away from your Talk. Using gross or highly offensive images to prove a point might backfire. I remember being in an audience and witnessing a man give a Talk where he used an animation of a child being held at gun point and crying. For many reasons, this was a bad idea but what made it worse was that it was around the time that there was an increase in school shootings. Those images were an emotional triggered for the audience and there was absolutely nothing he could do or say in that moment to win that audience.

- Avoid having wordy PowerPoints or misspellings; people will start to read your slides and if they have to edit them too they'll become disconnected from your Talk.

- If you are using handouts, make sure they are relevant, match your presentation format and easy to follow. Some handouts are best used if passed out after the Talk to take as references.

For lovers of all things performing arts like myself there is nothing more thrilling than the moment you stand on the stage. Rather your stage is millions of people or a one-on-one conversation managing the moment is about maximizing the time and the message. You manage your moments when you recognize the value of every second and making every word count. The average commercial runs 15-30 seconds. In that small amount of time the Marketing department is challenged to convey a big message about a business and or a product. That's why I believe that regardless of how much time you are given when you manage the moment you can convey the message. Most speakers are given more time than that of a commercial and with more time comes more responsibility. I have viewed many of my Talks from how I started to how I ended up presenting and I realized that I've never delivered a Talk from the perspective of the first draft. Every Talk evolved into something much bigger and better. Why? Because my original thoughts were cultivated in time, various coaching and life experiences matured my perspectives and I simply grew as a writer. So in the very moment that I stand on the stage all of that experience and growth comes rushing to my head. In that moment I want to share everything but I am challenged to manage the moment and the information that I release.


## Deliver the Talk

The United States 1st amendment gives us the right to speech while the 5th amendment gives us the right to remain silent. The heart of the matter is to know when to implement the appropriate amendment in life and on the stage. The right to speak also comes with the responsibility for what you speak. Like it, love it or hate it! The social media platform of uncensored public opinion is here and it can make or break you. Believe it or not your everyday person with a social media account has an audience and the potential to influence that audience.

Because of the vast stretch of the internet, a video of something you said could go viral before you even leave the stage. People will negligently start sharing and making comments around an excerpt or even worse an edited part of your Talk without even knowing the surrounding content. Although there is a legal and or perceived right to privacy those rights have been violated more times than one would like to admit and in some cases, our legal system has not caught up with technology. When on the stage it is best to remember that you are ALWAYS in the PUBLIC even when you are in a PRIVATE setting. There is ALWAYS a camera rolling, a tape recording and/or a malice ear listening to create mischief. I didn't say that to induce fear I said it to keep you aware. Taking the stage comes with embracing vulnerability. You have to stand on the stage as if the world is watching & listening because with the vast amount of technology and all the "go live" options, people all over the world just might be watching and listening. We all love a kind audience and an easy Talk but that's not always the case. Sometimes you are presented with:

## Difficult Talks

Not all difficult Talk s are controversial in nature; some might just be a hard sells pitch, or an academically challenging subject. However, when delivering Talks that are controversial or sensitive topics your delivery is of most importance. Delivering an already difficult topic with arrogance and or anger only intensifies the conflict. When you take the stage you are accountable for your audience. As a responsible speaker your aim should never be to incite riot or cause mayhem. When delivering a difficult Talk a responsible speaker's goal is to present their perspective and/or evidence with a technique and compassionate care. Especially if the speaker is looking to persuade or call an audience to action regard an issue.

## Difficult Audience

I would like to believe that every time I present a Talk, I'm presenting to an audience that cares and agrees with me but I know that's not always the case. Standing before people can be a very arduous task but it's even more problematic when you have to stand before people that are opposed to what you are presenting. This type of audience tends to show their resistance through their body language and facial expressions. As a speaker, it's okay to acknowledge this and assure your audience that you understand their feelings; assure them that you value their time and that you appreciate their attendance. Try to engage the audience as much as possible and if applicable, provide a space for Q&A.

Honestly, there was a time or two that I didn't pass the test of handling a difficult audience professionally. I remember one time I was speaking in a small basement area and a senior citizen lady who was known to be very loud and rude was just that as I began to do my Talk. At first I tried to ignore her in hopes that she would implement some self-control but she didn't so I simply stopped talking and I just stared at her. It was awkward and I would never suggest that a speaker does that but it worked; she realized that she was too loud and stopped talking. However, here is where I went wrong in the situation; instead of moving on I begin to talk "not so subliminally" about how it doesn't matter how old you are; everybody should show respect. I had clearly allowed the situation to shift my focus; completely ignoring the rest of my audience and what I was there to do. Eventually I gained my focus back but unfortunately I had already made myself look like the bully speaker picking on the little old senior citizen lady in the audience. Months after that Talk I attempted to justify my response to that situation but clearly there was no justification for my actions; I was wrong.

Whatever you do, maintain your composure never let your audience see you sweat or lose your cool. Never abuse your position on the stage by using your microphone as a weapon. Be kind even when or if the audience is not. Remember who you are and the self-presentation that you are trying to represent; let it be said that you remained calm and that you handled yourself and the situation professionally.

## Combative Audiences

Safety is always first; if you do not feel safe you shouldn't take the stage. However, if the situation does not seem that serious and you want to proceed you should prepare yourself for potential outbursts or in this day and age the social media backlash and slander. People can be mean and words do hurt. You have to remember that as strong as your conviction is regarding your subject someone in your audience might be a strong advocate against it.

# Stage 7:

## Post Stage

### The Moments After

You could have delivered the perfect Talk but your mind will tell you that you missed something and or it will magnify that one little moment that you stumbled over your words; it's inevitable and it happens to the best of us. There will be times that people rush up to you after you leave the stage and tell you how great you are and how much your Talk helped their life. Those are the feel good moments; appreciate them and the people that took the time to encourage you. Normally when I leave the stage there is a litany of emotions that I experience. I'll usually find someone to hug really tight in an attempt to release the residue of energy. Depending on the subject I may find a quiet space and shed a few tears as a form of release. After my TEDx Columbus Talk I remember hugging my coach Megan as the tears began to flow from my eyes. Megan looked at me and said "Tamekia, you've come a long way from your grandmother's bathroom" and of course that revelation made me cry even more because in that moment, I was reminded that not all tears represent pain; some embody the fullness of victory.

### The People Factor

The truth is that you don't have to love or care about people to take the stage. In fact I've seen countless Talks presented that lacked compassion and you could tell that the speaker could care less about the audience. I've seen Talks where the goal was to "get it over with" and the ultimate goal was to never "doing it again". While I can understand that school of thought from a person that was being forced to speak that could never be the mindset of a person that passion for the stage. A person that sees the stage as a career or a calling has to authentically love and operate from a place of compassionate care. I've never seen or experienced a great speaker that didn't passion.

Loving people will help you resist discouragement when some people for no real reason at all hate you. One day I was on social media and I began to read some of the comments that people wrote on a celebrity's page. The celebrity was publically exposed for an indiscretion in his personal life. I was extremely shocked at the level of hate that people felt so comfortable publically displaying. The words were vicious even to the point of wishing the celebrity would die a violent death. It made me realize that the same people that at one point "liked" him enough to follow him now declared their disappointment and hate for him. Unfortunately, this is life and it can happen to the best of us. You can have every intention to do well and then make one bad decision and all of a sudden people will leave you and share the news of your failure. However, the ability to love people is wrapped in forgiveness and that's why it is so necessary to have love. As a speaker you will almost never get a 100% approval rating no matter how well you execute a Talk. Audiences are made up of people and people are different; some will agree, some will disagree and some will be converted either way. Some people will not give you a standing ovation even if you deserve one; others will fold their arms and refuse to clap for you. And because of your race, gender and or ethnicity some people will always believe that you shouldn't even have the opportunity to take the stage. The good news is that you don't need everyones' approval; nor do you have to allow their negative words to determine how you feel about you. People will love you, people will hate you; people will love the fact that they hate you and hate the fact that they love you; that's just the people factor. The source of your strength and the determination to keep going has to come from within and when you need it you have to pull it out of yourself. If you give that power to people they will take your strength every time you do or say something they don't like. Loving people does not mean that you allow people to use and manipulate you. There will always be a small remnant of people that will stick by your side. Don't allow that small number to discourage you because the remnant is about quality not quantity.

## What's Next?

I don't care what you achieve in life the question of "what's next" will always be the question that follows that achievement. Sometimes this can feel a bit overwhelming especially if you don't have an answer. However, when you know who you are you will recognize the opportunity in that question. Answering that question is like being a gifted painter with a blank canvas because your answer gives you the freedom to create something great out of nothing. Some people would say hurry and do something else and build on the momentum and other would say be still and listen for direction. Personally I fall somewhere in the middle with my advice because I believe both of those things are necessary. Some speakers would love to do one Talk and become an overnight sensation while others if they impacted one person's life their mission would be accomplished.

At the rehearsal of my TED Talk in Vancouver I remember sitting off stage by myself just thinking about "what's next" and I must have been in really deep thought because Cloe (and employee at TED) asked: "Are you alright?" I remember telling her that I was sitting there trying to figure out my whole life at which point we both laughed but certainly there was some honesty in my joke. I'm a creative but I'm also an entrepreneur and both of those qualities have been at times my vice and my virtue. There were times I would be irritated at myself for even having the audacity to "dream out loud." In my discouragement I remember wondering why I couldn't just be content with being regular, working a regular job and living a regular life! And then it happened; after being in Canada and taking the stage at the TED Conference I returned to living my regular life at my regular job and if it's at all possible to be grateful and dejected simultaneously that would have described me perfectly. I loved the culture and the services that my department provided but it wasn't the stage and I wasn't creating. Nevertheless, I had enough wisdom to know that I couldn't make unwise or hasty decisions out of my emotions. I knew that the days and months to come would be critical and I would have to prepare day and night to create a new narrative for my life. So in my distress I did what I know to do; I began to write and ironically enough when it was all said and done my writing ended up being this book. And now I'm thinking; what's next?